Utah State Capitol

Salt Lake City

Jane Moorman

There is a saying, "It was a Friday night and it seemed like a good idea at the time." That sums up the beginning of the State Capitols Project.

When I told my brother of my idea of photographing state capitols, he said, "You do know there are 50 states and two of them you can't drive to."

Each capitol has its own unique beauty that reflects the state's personality when it was built.

Jane Moorman, photographer

Utah: the Beehive State

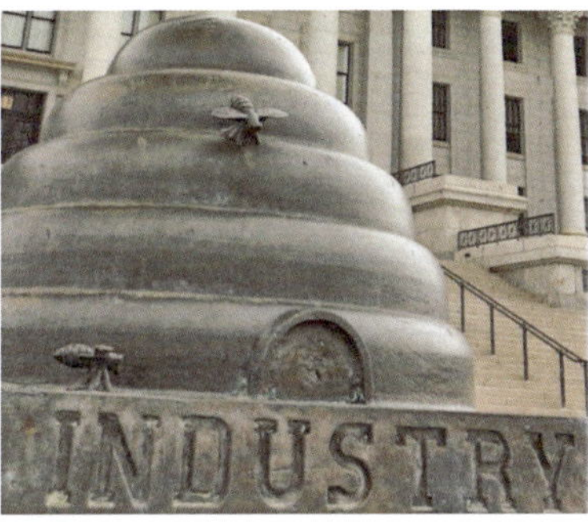

Mormonism has had a significant impact in shaping Utah's history and destiny for which no other state can make such a claim.

Since the westward migration of the Mormons into the Great Salt Lake Valley in 1847, when Brigham Young declared "This is the place," the development and progress of Utah has been dominat ed by the influence of the Church of Jesus Christ Latter Day Saints.

It took 50 years for the area settled by the Mor mons to become a state. In 1849 the pioneers adopted a provisional government and constitution in naming their state Deseret, a term that originated in the Book of Mormon and is said to mean honeybees.

Before the U.S. Congress agreed to grant statehood in 1896, the provisional government had to change its name to Territory of Utah and decrease its boundaries which included parts of nine current states - Utah, Nevada, Arizona, Idaho, Colorado, Wyoming, New Mexico, Oregon and southern California.

Several attempts at statehood also failed, primarily because of the LDS church's stance on polygamy. In 1890, the church officially aban doned the practice and remove it from its doctrine.

Several buildings in Salt Lake City served as tempo rary homes for the state legislature and offices for state officers, until it was determined that the the space was inadequate, and several local leaders and businessmen began to call for a new permanent capi tol building.

Architect Richard Klet ting's design was approved for its simple, dramatic an straightforward Neo clasical Revival plan for the 286-foot-tall state house. Construction began on Dec. 26, 1912, and the building was dedicated on Oct. 9, 1916.

Statue of Brigham Young.

Utah Capitol

Inspired by Classical architecture the early designs by architect Richard K.A. Kletting, were compared to Greece's Parthenon.

Constructed of Utah granite, mined in nearby Little Cottonwood Canyon, the building is 404 feet long, 240 feet wide and the copper dome is 250 feet high.

Fifty-two Corinthian columns, each 32 feet tall by 3.5 feet in diameter sitting on an exposed foundation podium surround the south, east and west side of the capitol.

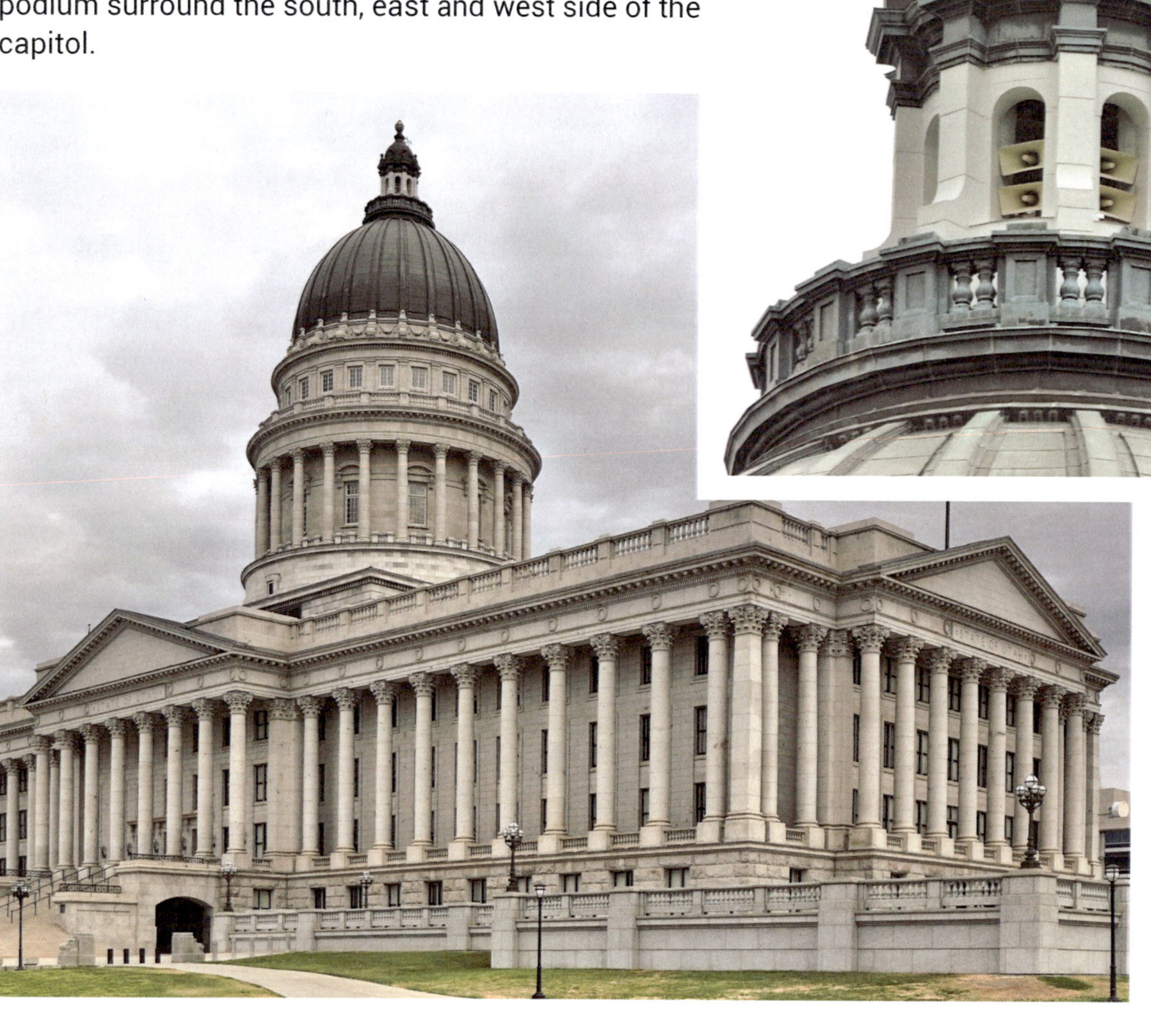

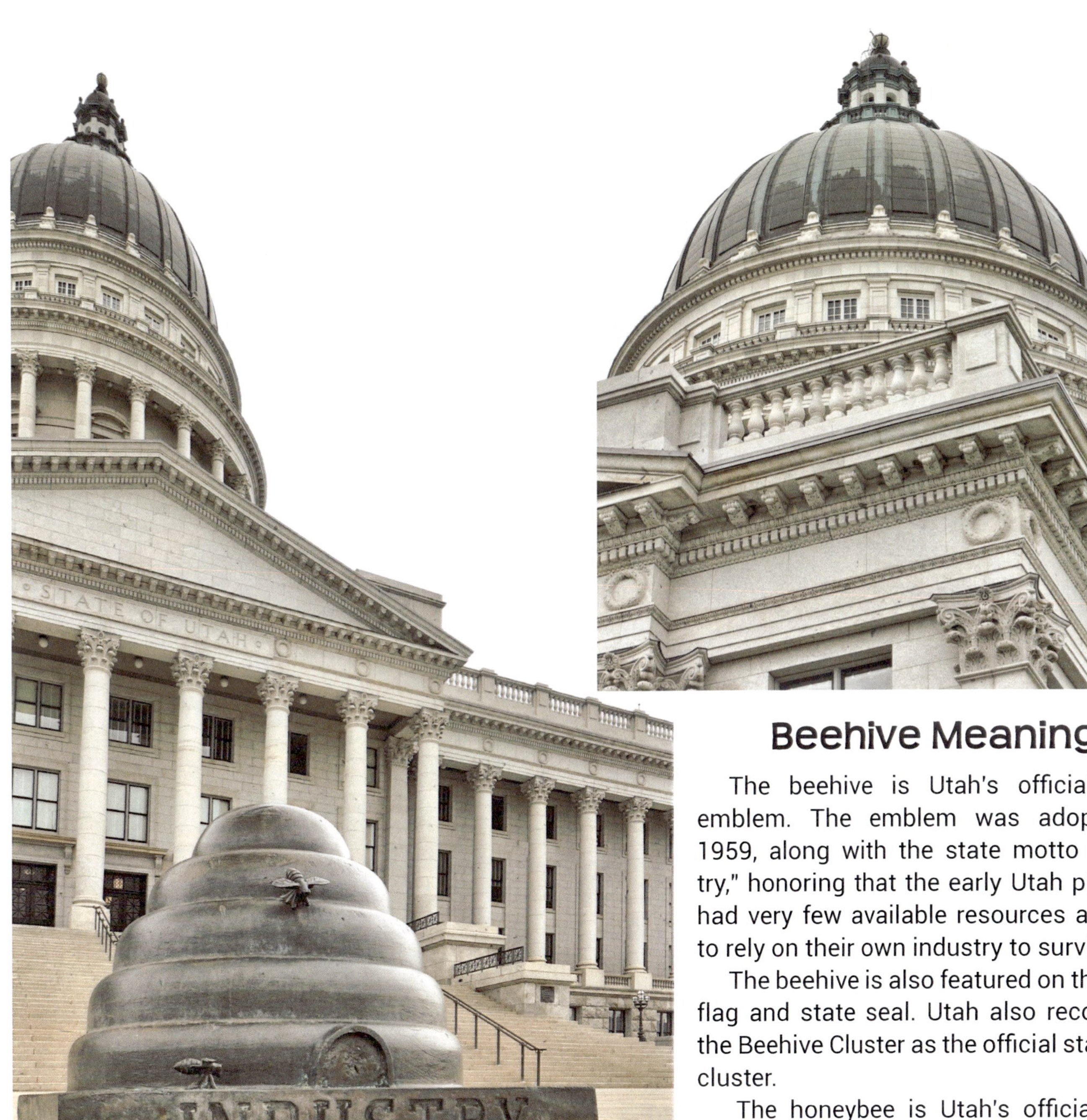

Beehive Meaning

The beehive is Utah's official state emblem. The emblem was adopted in 1959, along with the state motto "Industry," honoring that the early Utah pioneers had very few available resources and had to rely on their own industry to survive.

The beehive is also featured on the state flag and state seal. Utah also recognizes the Beehive Cluster as the official state star cluster.

The honeybee is Utah's official state insect.

Rotunda Dome

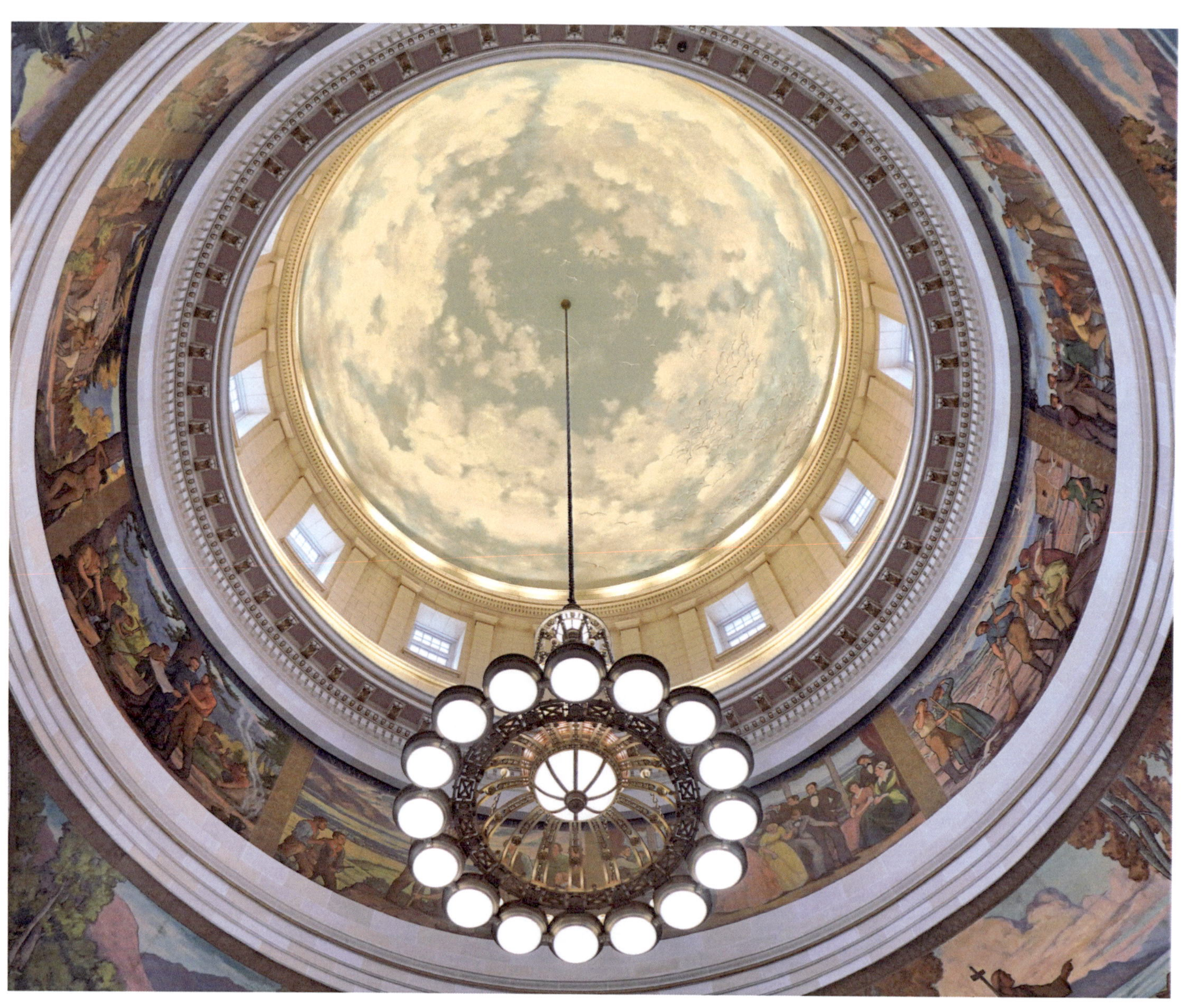

Rotunda Artwork

The capitol's rotunda pendentives 14x20 feet paintings illustrate the first non-native people known to have explored the territory that would become Utah.

Eash of these explorations left lasting contributions to Utah's modern geographic and cultural history.

The cyclorama that circles the dome contains more than 100 characters, many of whom are more than 10 feet tall, in eight scenes from Utah's history.

The two sets of paintings, by Greene, Cope, Midgley and Rasmussen, were part of a Civil Works Administration public works art project done in 1933-1935.

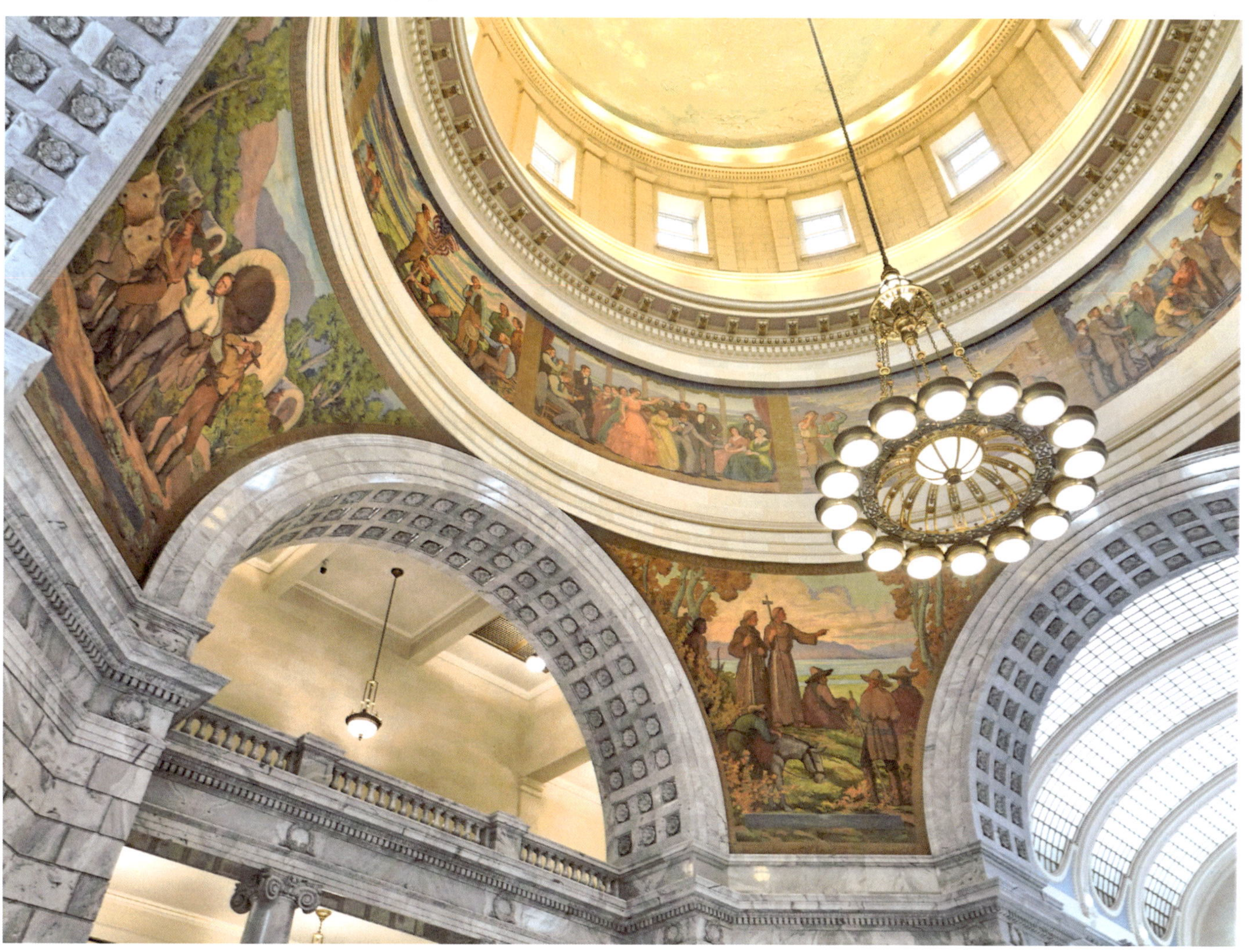

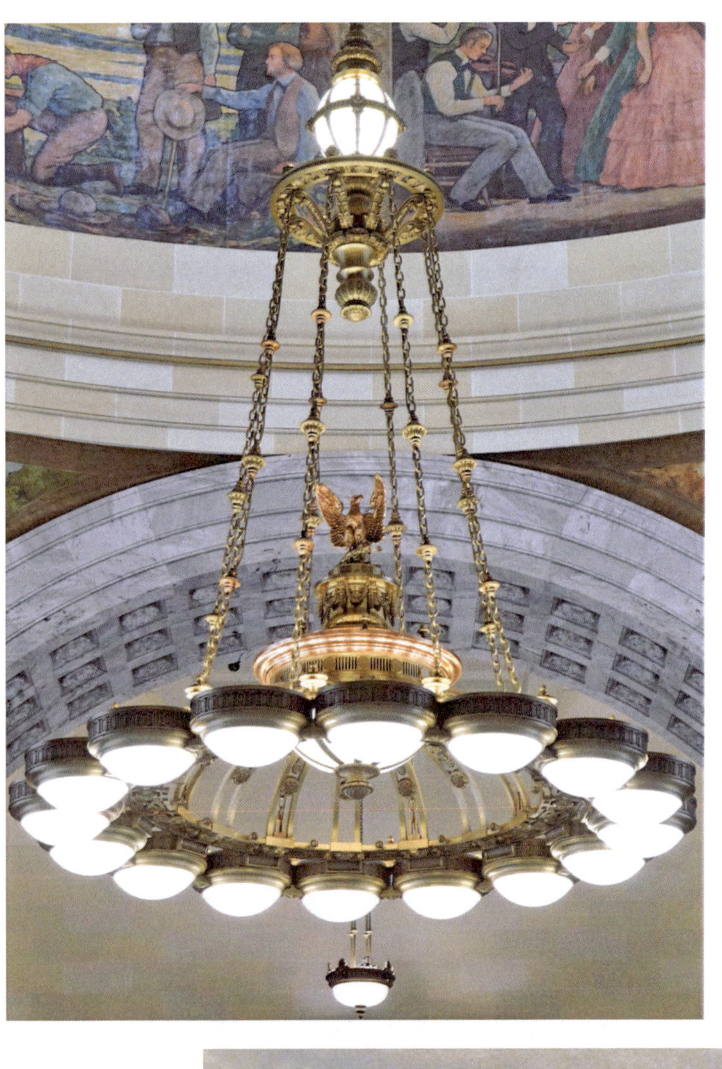

Utah's interior ceiling of the dome, which reaches 165 feet above the floor, is unique com pared to other state's capitol domes.

Artist William Slater's mural includes seagulls flying amongst clouds. The mural was chosen because the California gull is Utah's official state bird and represents the miracle of the gulls from Utah's history.

Seagulls saved the 1848 crops by eating thousands of insects that were devouring the pioneers' fields.

Suspended from the dome's ceiling is the origi nal chandelier weighing 3,000 pounds. The chain supporting it weighs an additional 1,000 pounds.

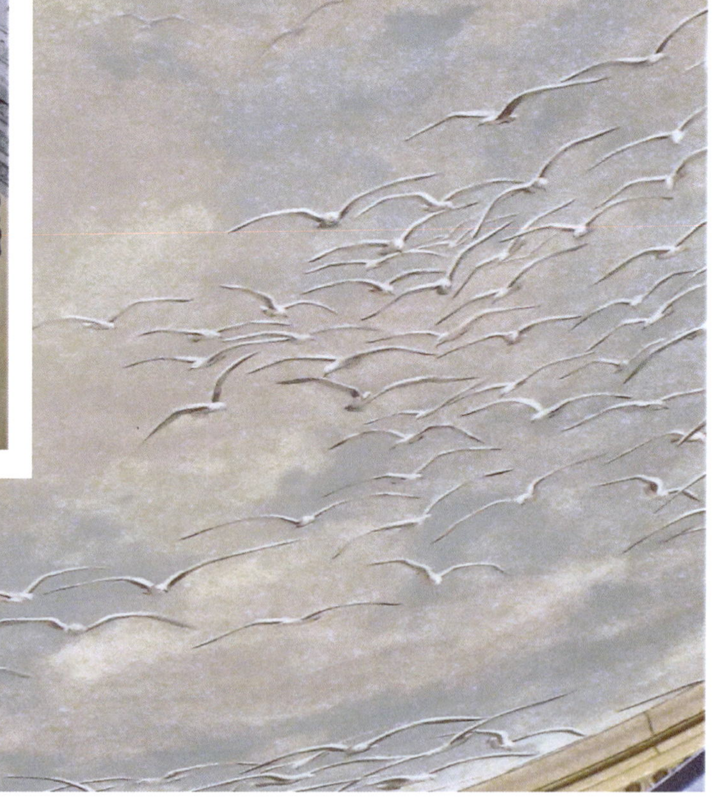

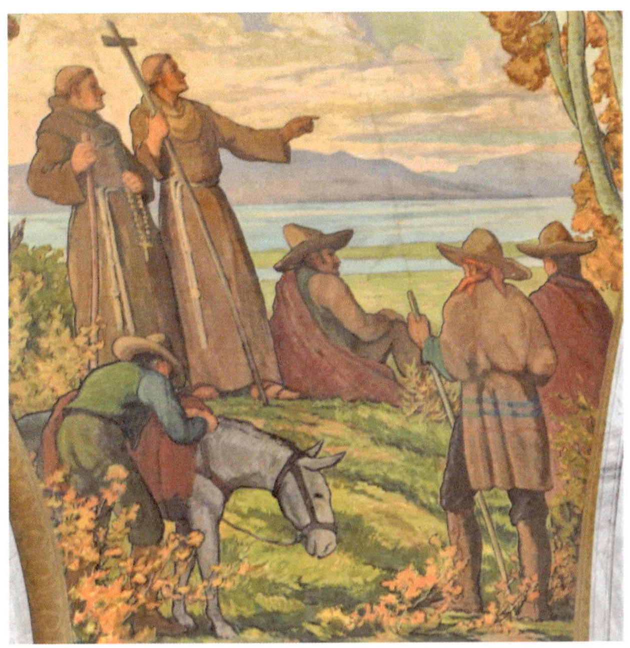

Father Escalante Discovers Utah Lake—1776

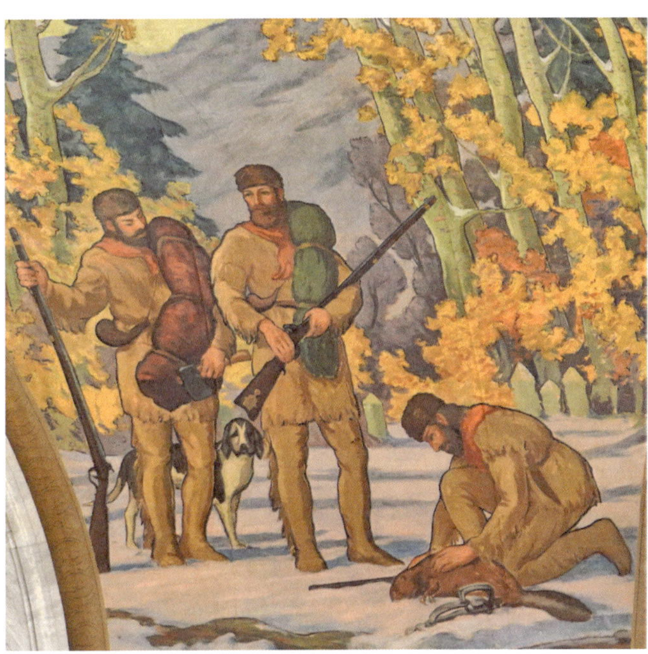

Peter Skene Ogden at Ogden River – 1828

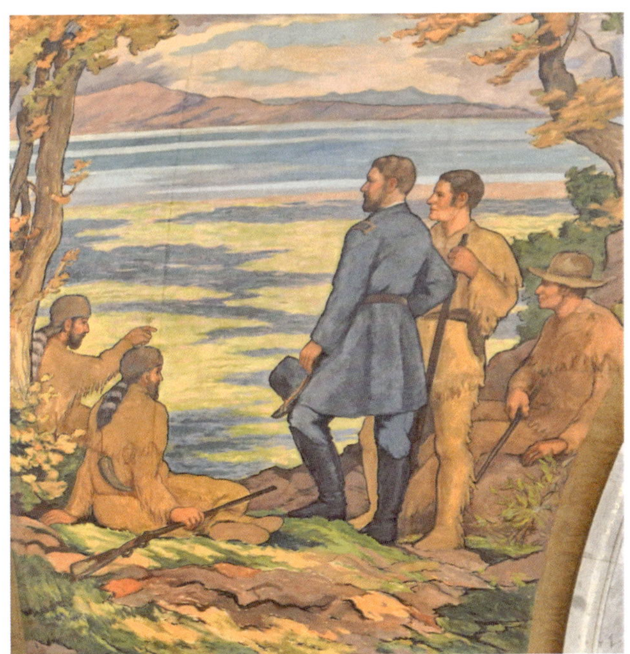

Fremont First Sees Great Salt Lake – 1843

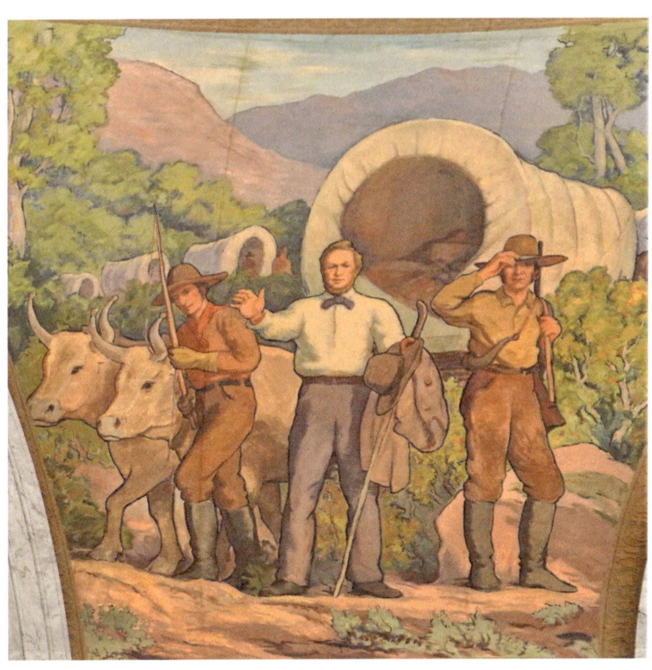

Brigham Young and Pioneers Entering the Valley – 1847

The Great Utahs

The 11-foot bronze sculptures created by artist Eugene Daub, Robert Firmin, and Jonah Hendrickson were added to the rotun da during the 2004-2008 resto ration.

Arts and Education depicts an adult muse offers educational guid ance to a child who represents the youth of Utah.

Science and Technology reminds the viewer of the impor-tance of past, present and future scientific and technological growth in Utah.

Immigration and Settlement symbolizes the value of welcoming new Utah citizens from all backgrounds.

Land and Community is unique among the niche sculp tures, as the youth is represent ed by a Rocky Mountain elk calf, which pauses on a mountain side, watched over by the spirit of an older man, the symbol of wisdom in the community

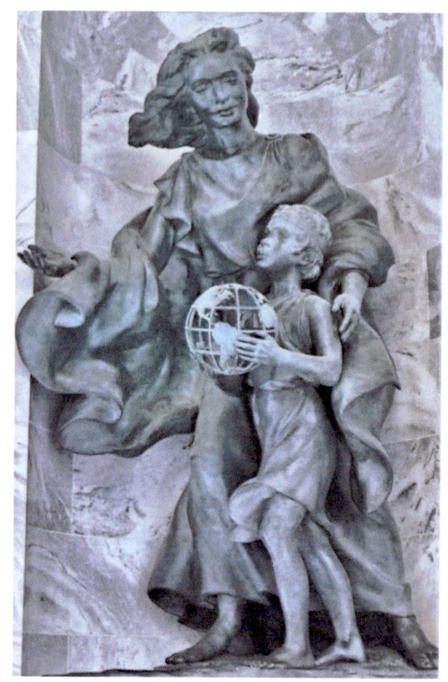

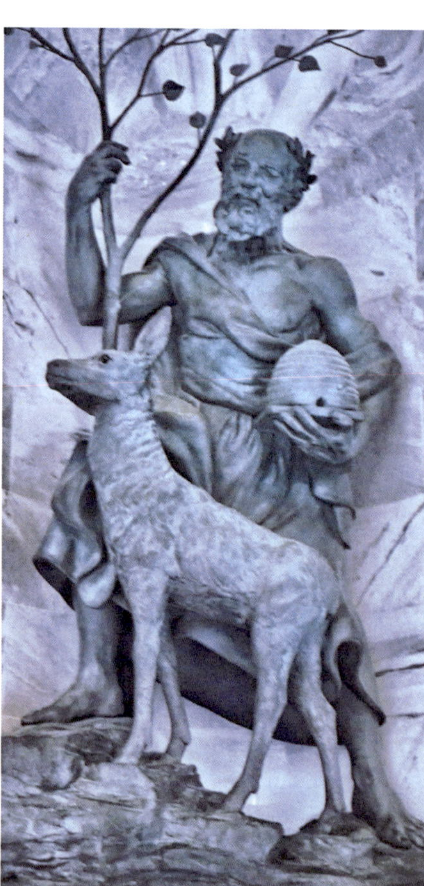

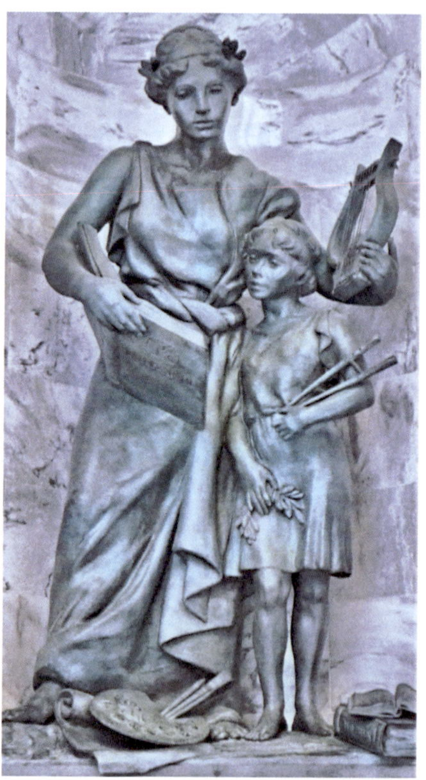

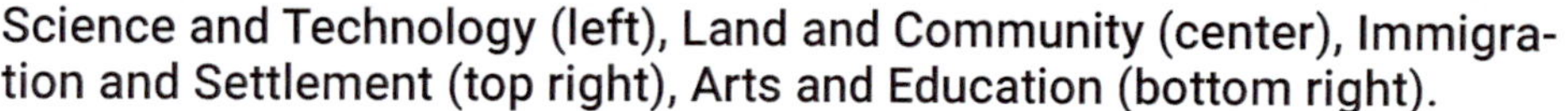

Science and Technology (left), Land and Community (center), Immigration and Settlement (top right), Arts and Education (bottom right).

Grand Staircase

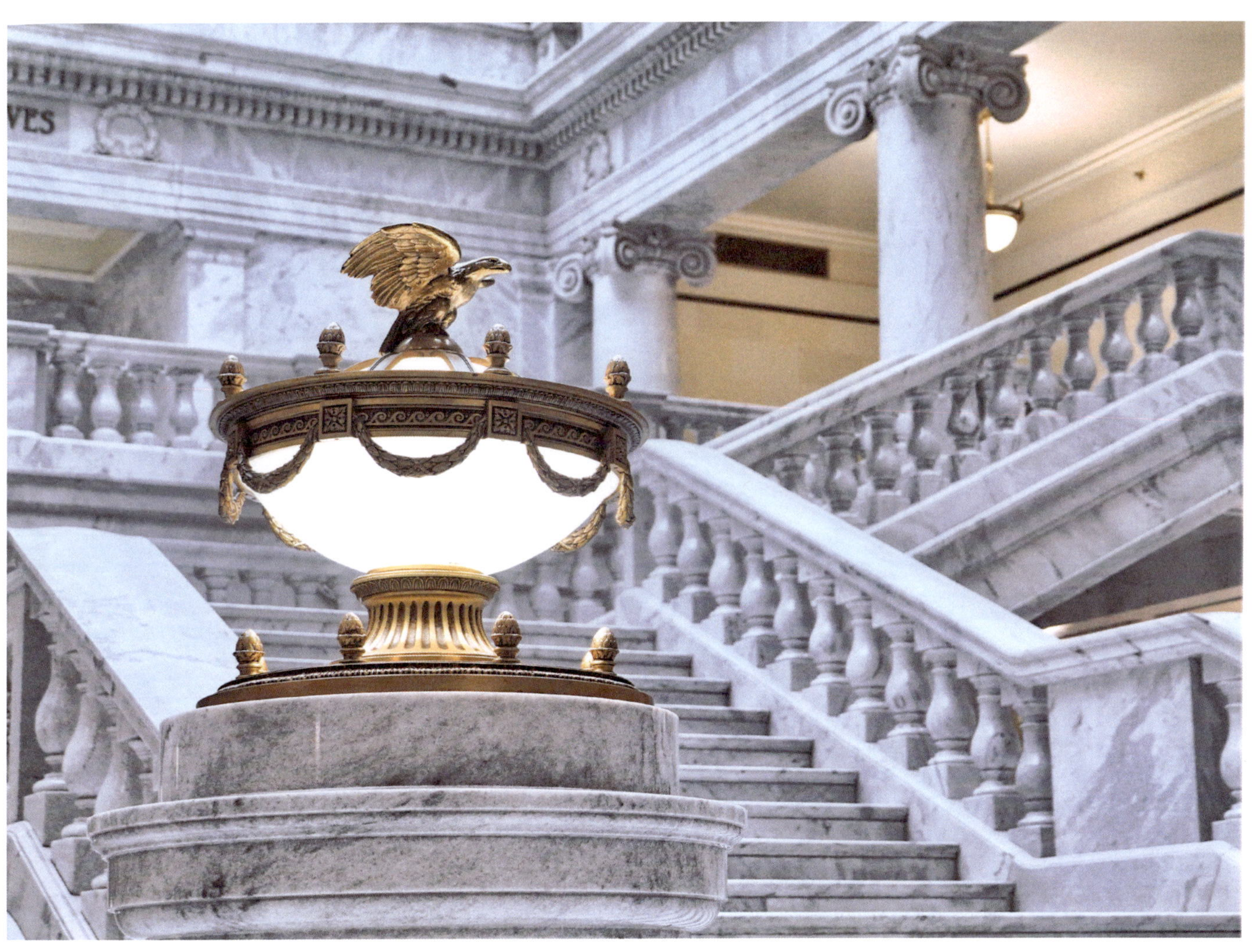

Legislative Wing Atrium

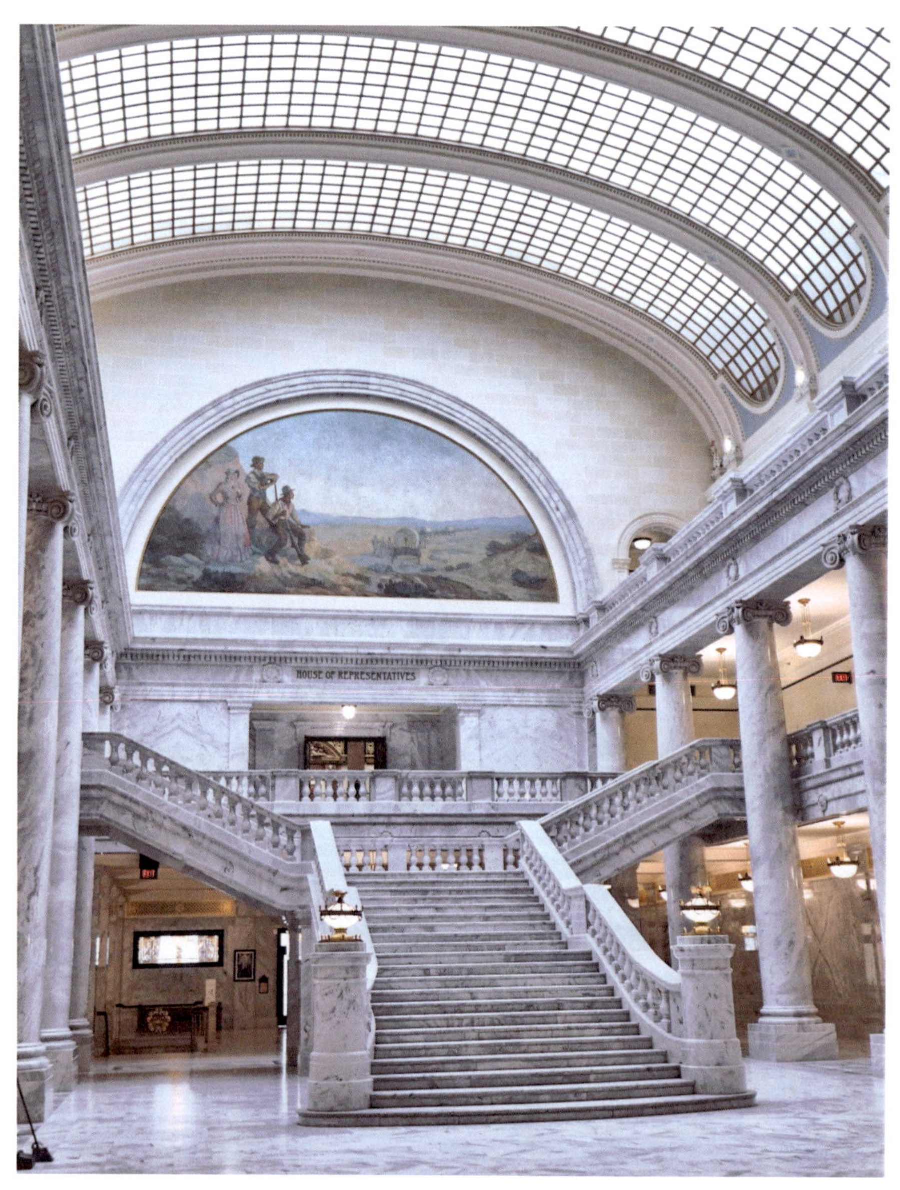

Atrium Artwork

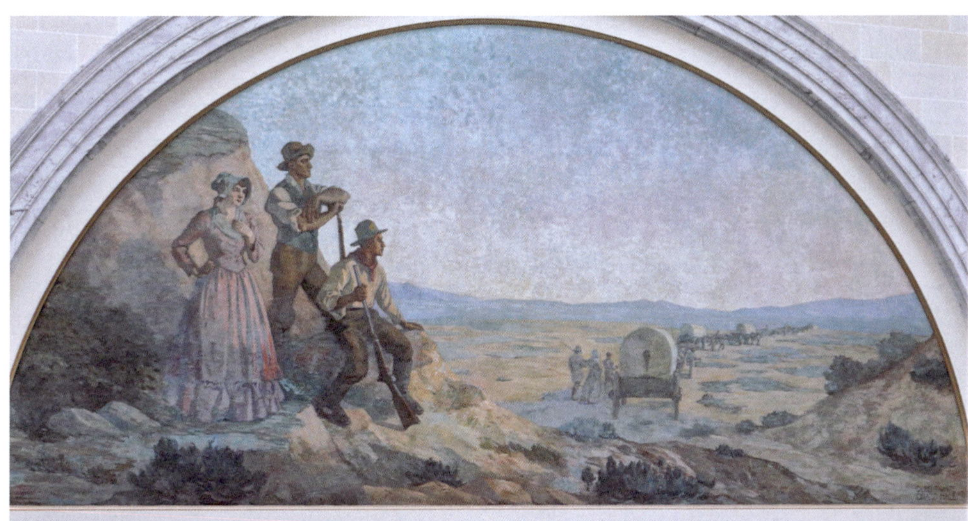

The Passing of the Wagons

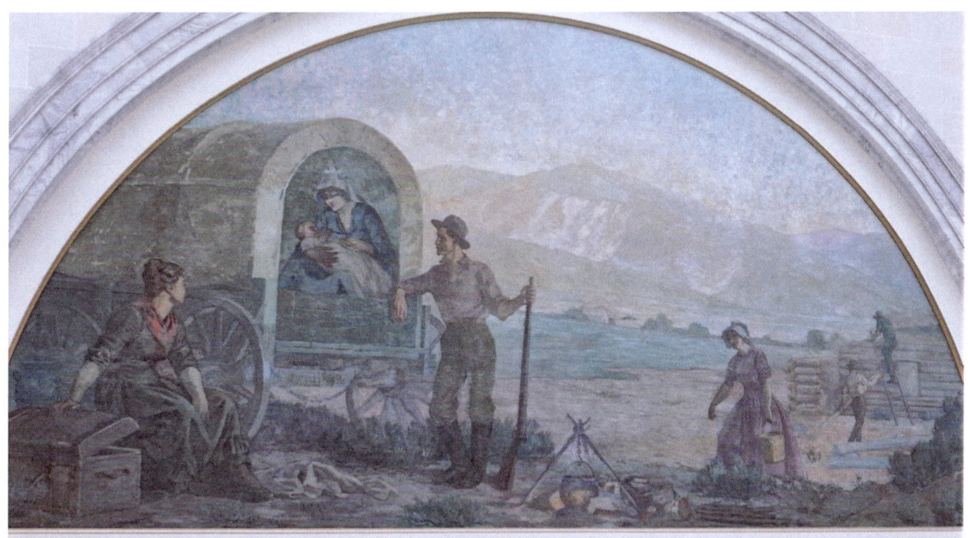

Madonna of the Wagon

Two of the first commissioned artworks in the capitol were installed in 1917 in the lunettes, at the end of the two grand atriums.

The 18 x 35 feet paint ings are by Girard Hale, of Utah, and Gilbert White, of New York.

Above the entrance to the House Chamber is the mural titled "Passing of the Wagons," which depicts the arrival of the pioneers in the Great Salt Lake Valley as first seen in July 1947.

"Madonna of the Wagon" is above the entrance to the Supreme Court. It depicts a mother with her infant child in a covered wagon with a family building their new home in the background.

The atriums flanking the east and west side of the rotunda contain large skylights, allowing sunlight to enter the two-story public area.

Gold Room

The state reception room, also known as the gold room, is often used to enter tain visiting dignitaries.

The room gets its name from the extensive usage of gold leaf in its decoration.

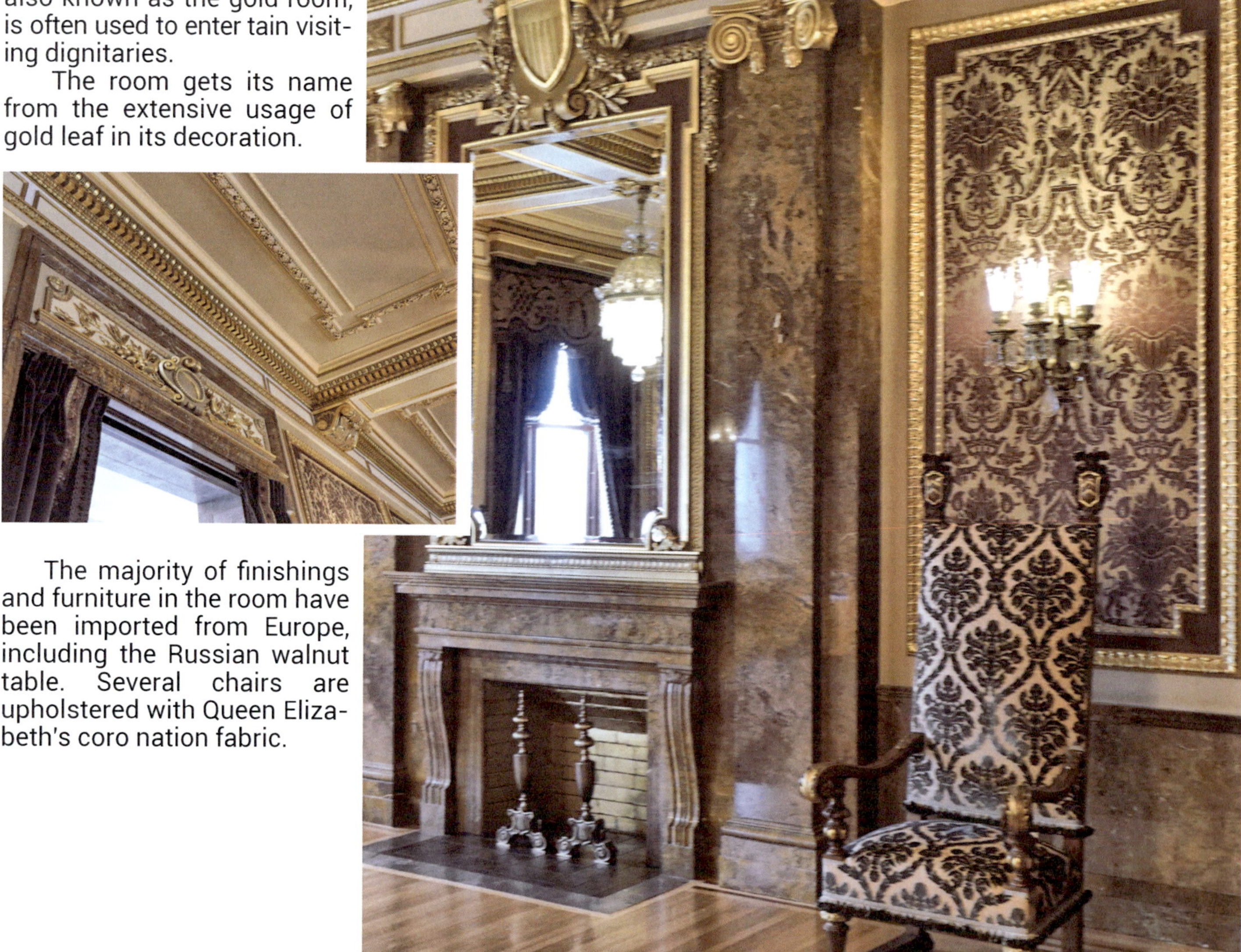

The majority of finishings and furniture in the room have been imported from Europe, including the Russian walnut table. Several chairs are upholstered with Queen Elizabeth's coro nation fabric.

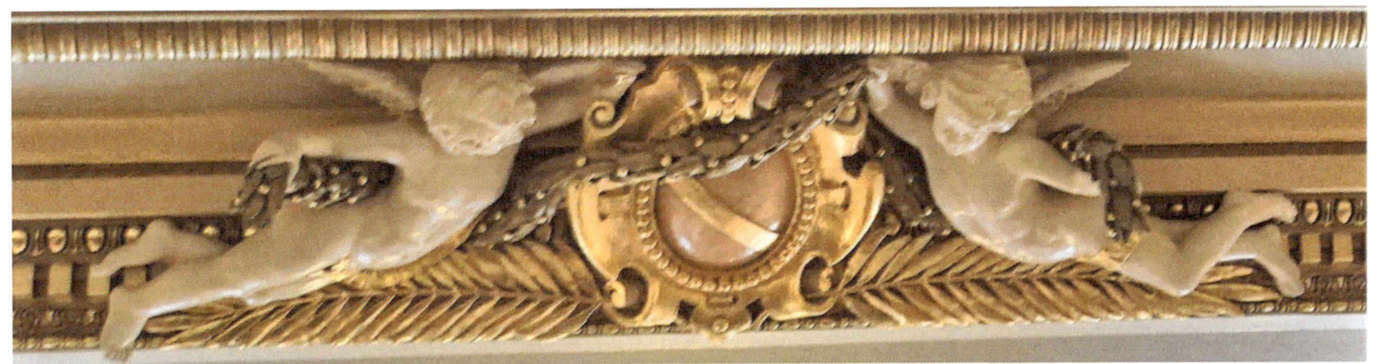

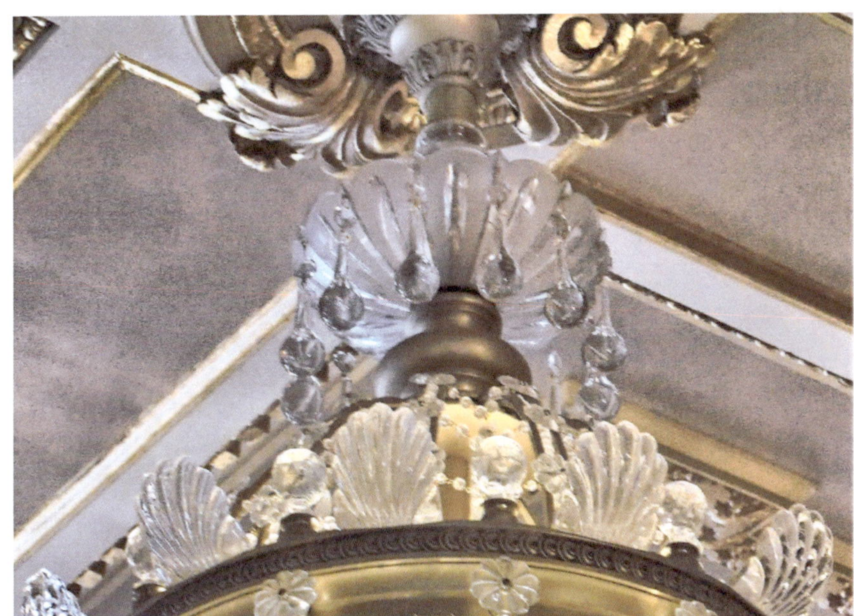

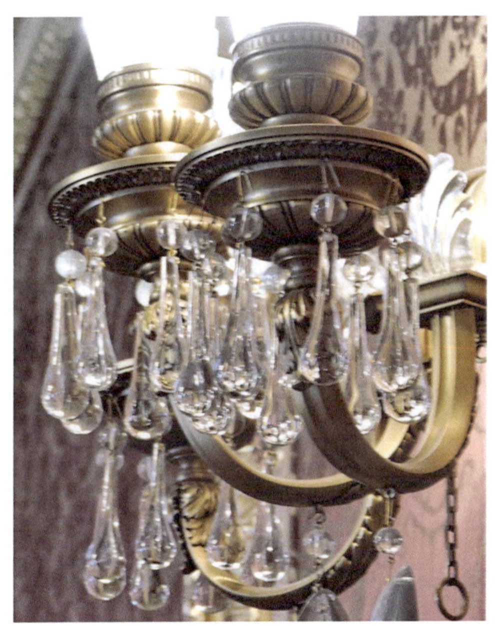

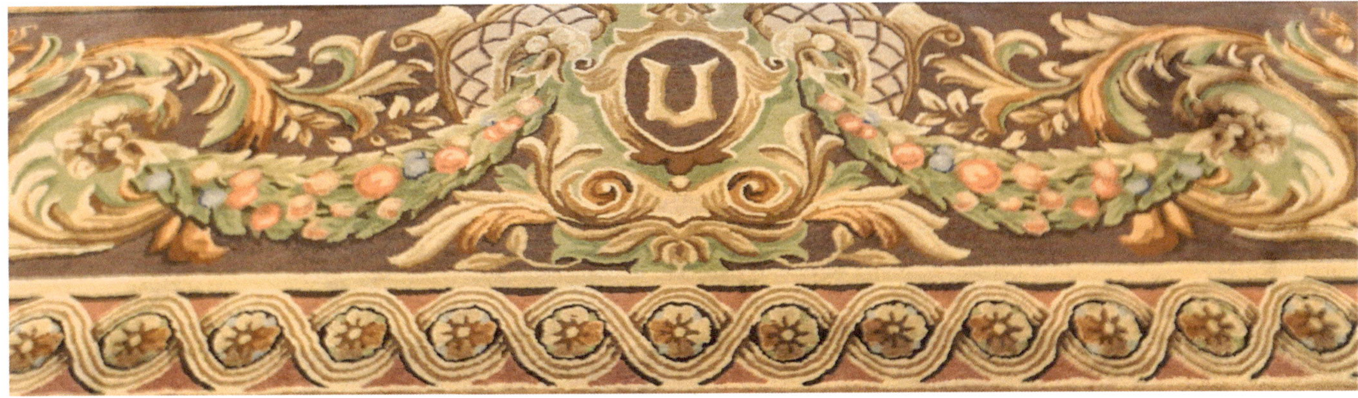

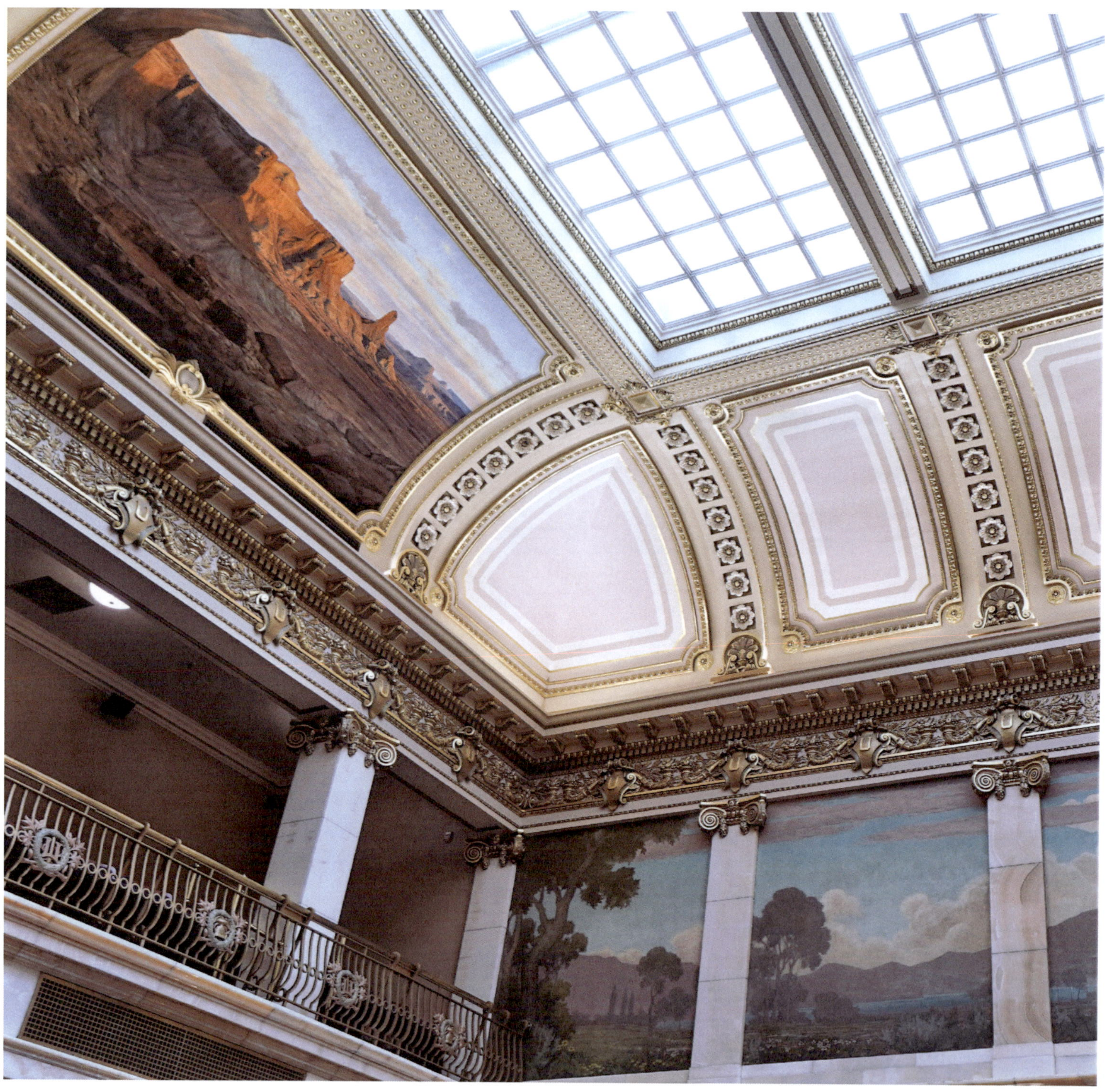

Senate Chamber

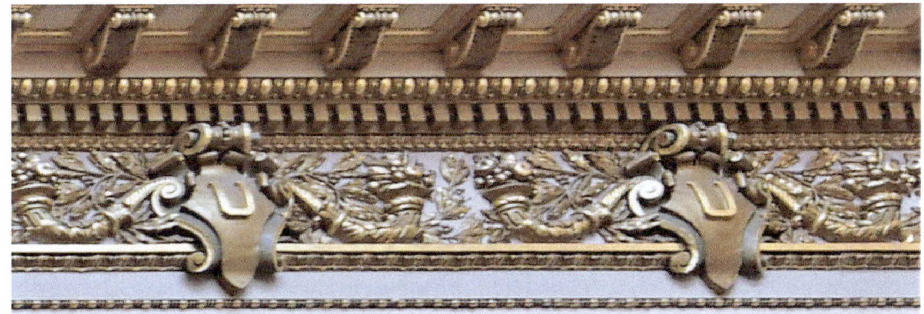

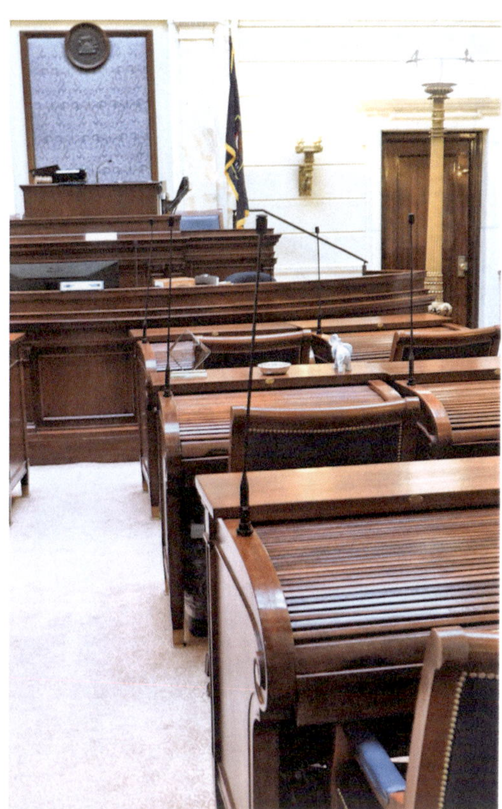

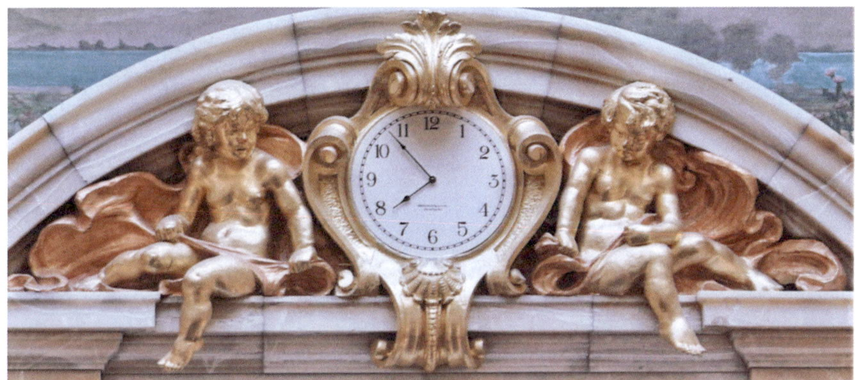

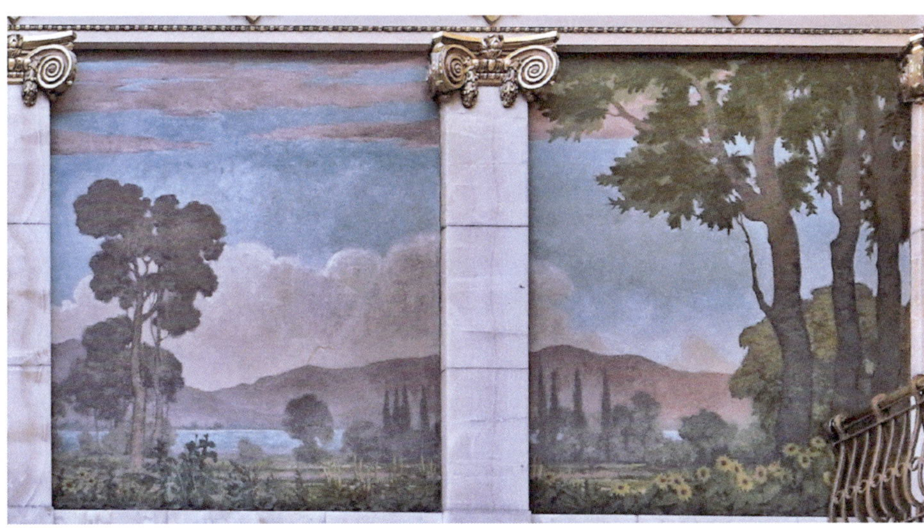

House of Representatives Chamber

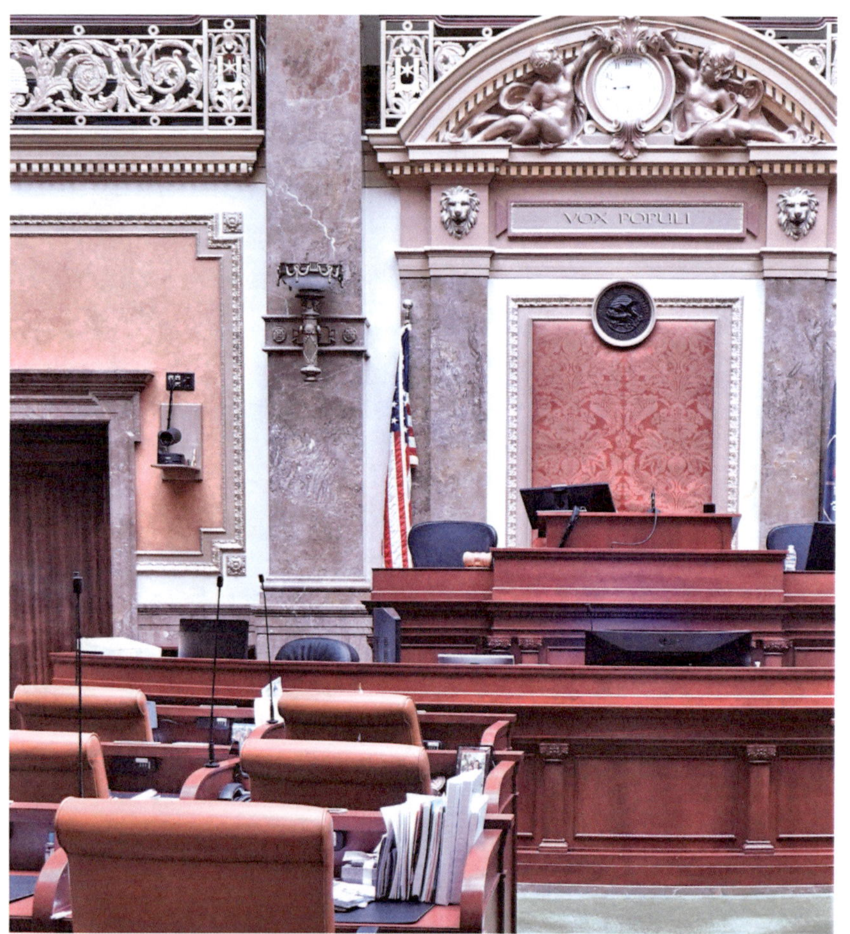

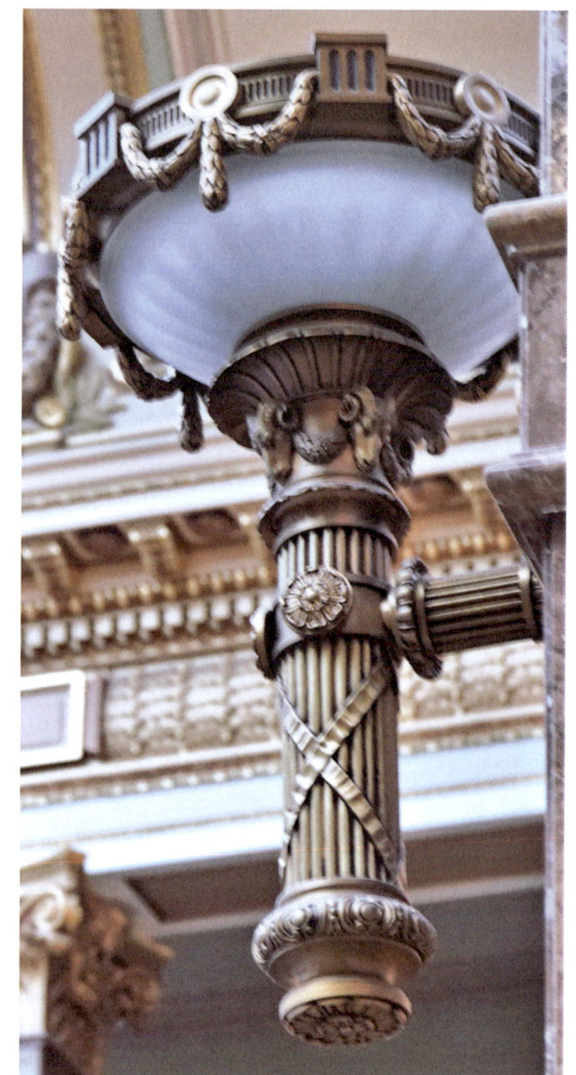

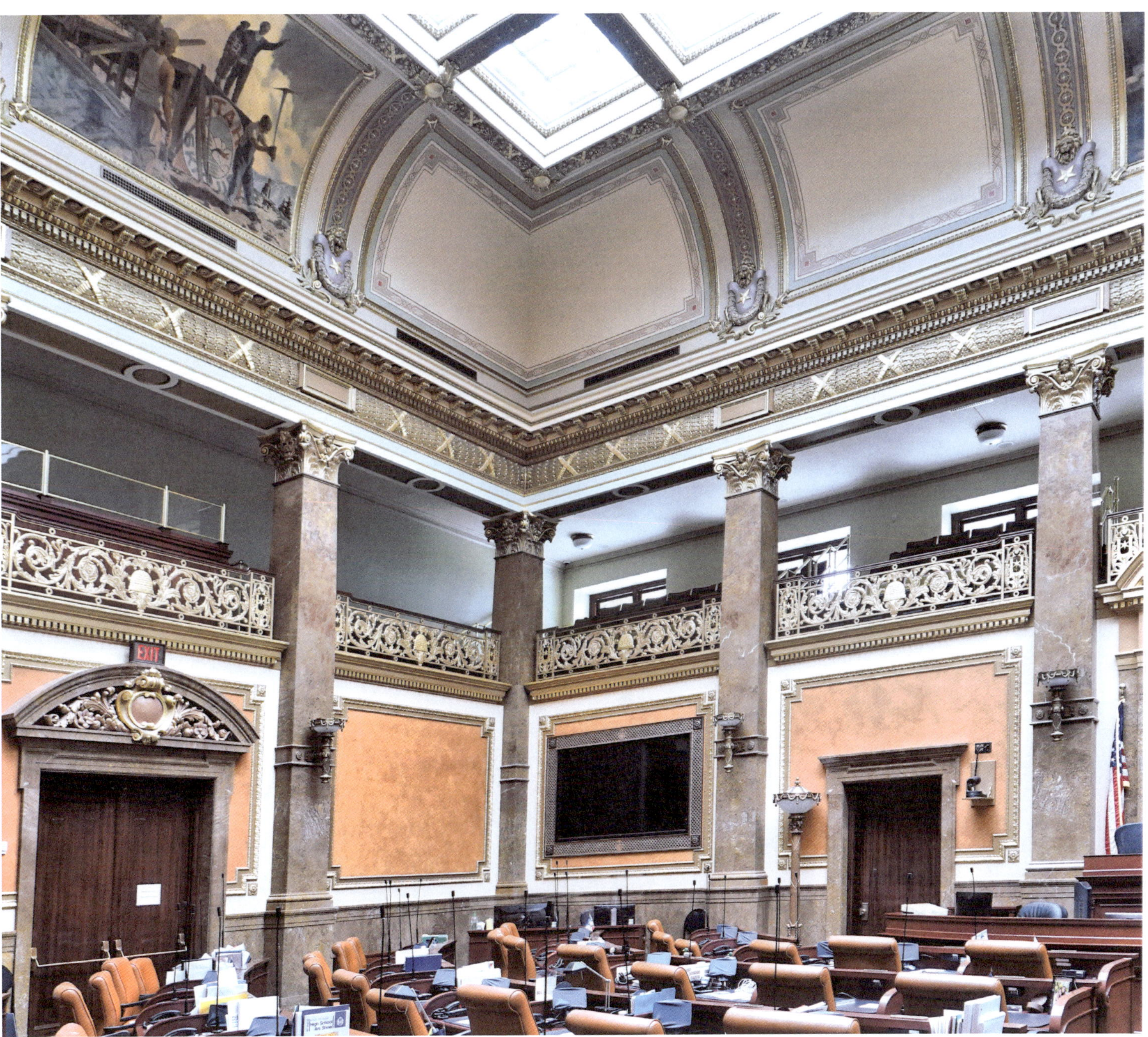

Unique Wall Patterns

Georgia marble wall panels are cut in book-cuts creating unique symmetrical patterns.

Columns of the Georgia marble also have surprising patterns.

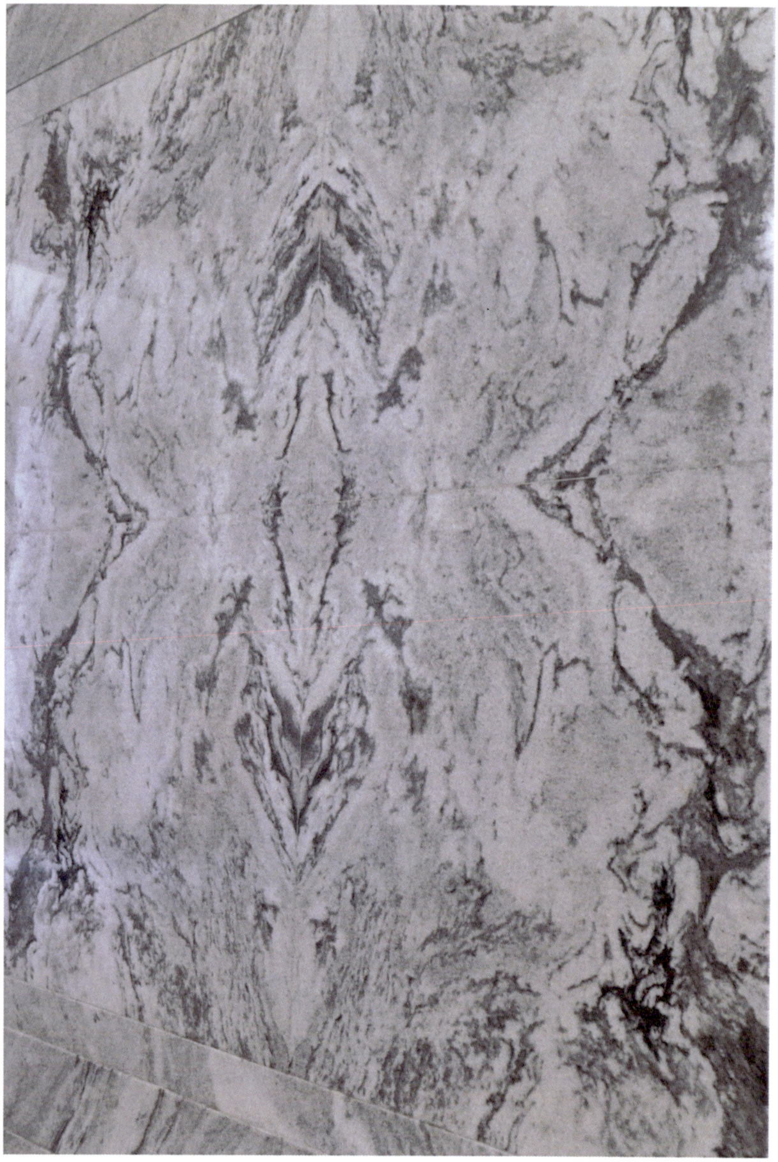

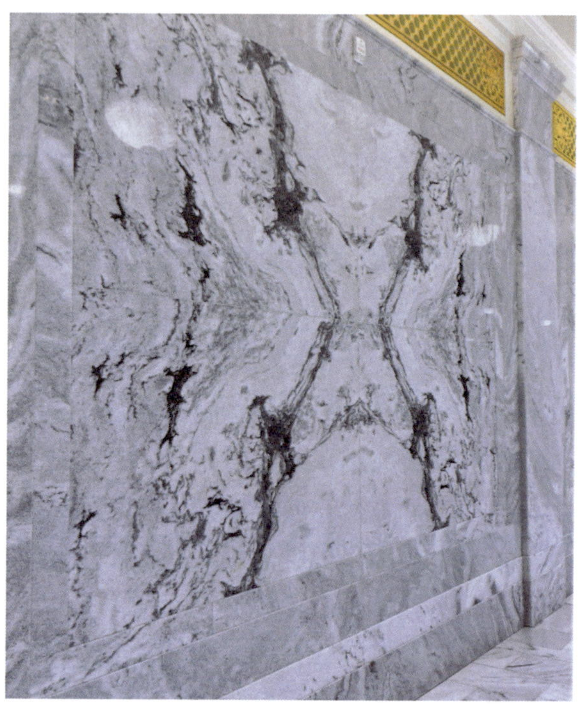

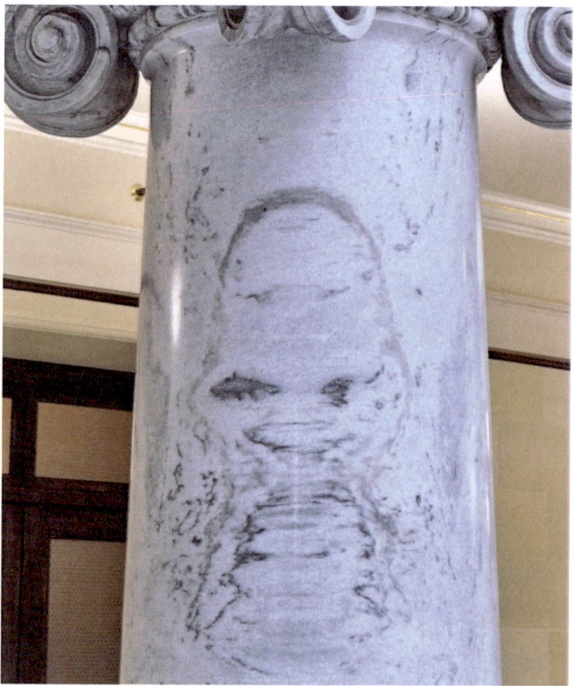

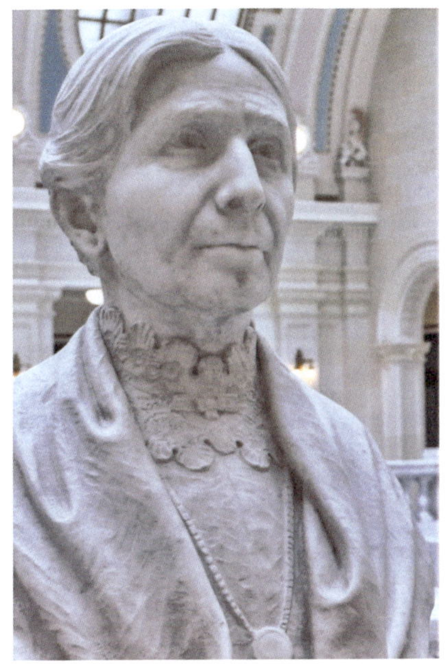

Emmeline B. Wells

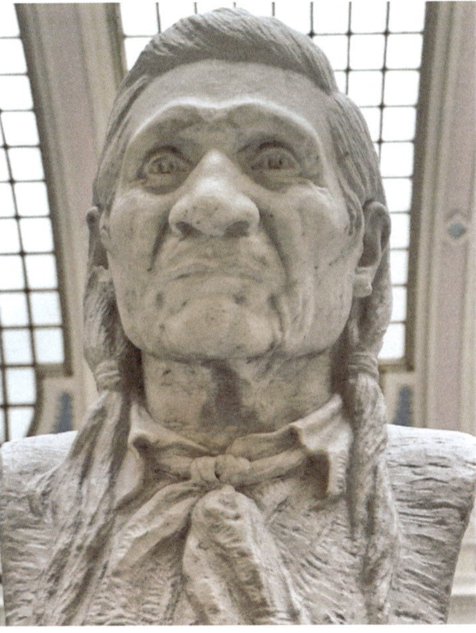

Unca Sam

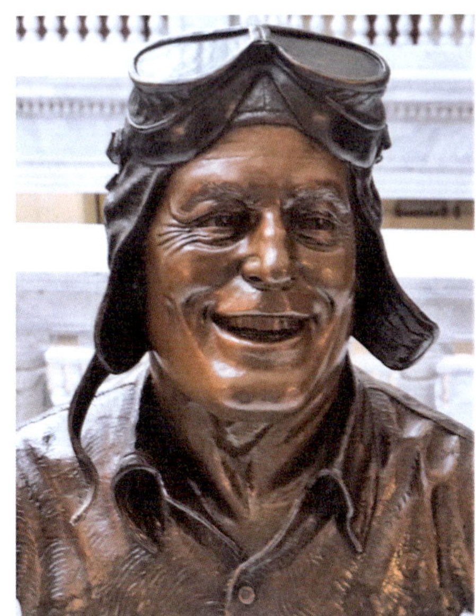

David Abbot 'Ab' Jenkins

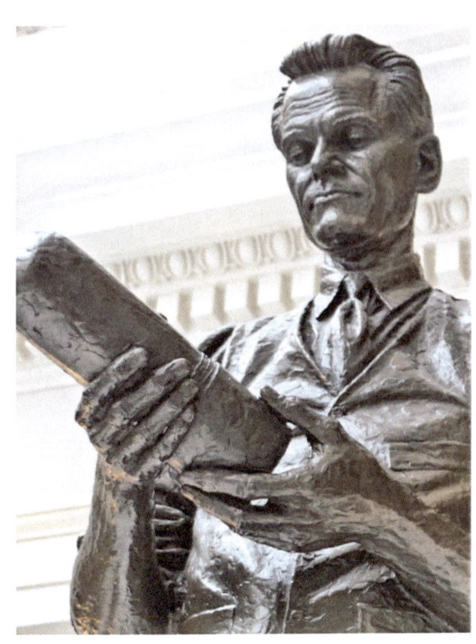

Philo Farnsworth

After the 2004-2008 Capitol restoration, the fourth floor returned to architect Kletting's original plans, and now includes expansive gallery space overlooking the rotunda.

Included are statues of Utah citizens who impacted history. Among them are:

Emmeline B. Wells remembered for her work as a journalist, poet and women's rights advocate.

Unca Sam a Ute Indian member of a peace missions sent to Washington, D.C. to negotiate with the federal government after the Meeker Massacre in Colorado in 1879.

David Abbot 'Ab' Jenkins a race car driver who set that world speed record of 161.18 mph on Utah's Bonneville Salt Flats.

Philo T. Farnsworth, inventor that developed the first completely electric television, and a nuclear fusion device that was very influential in the world of nuclear energy.

Utah's State Seal

The beehive featured in the center of the great seal of Utah is a symbol of hard work and industry.

The date 1847 is the year the Mormons came to Utah. 1896 is the year Utah became the 45th state.

A bald eagle, the United States national bird, perches atop the shield as a symbol of protection in peace and war.

The sego lilies on both sides of the beehive is the state flower. They are a symbol of peace.

The U.S. flag appears on each side of the shield representing Utah's support to the nation.

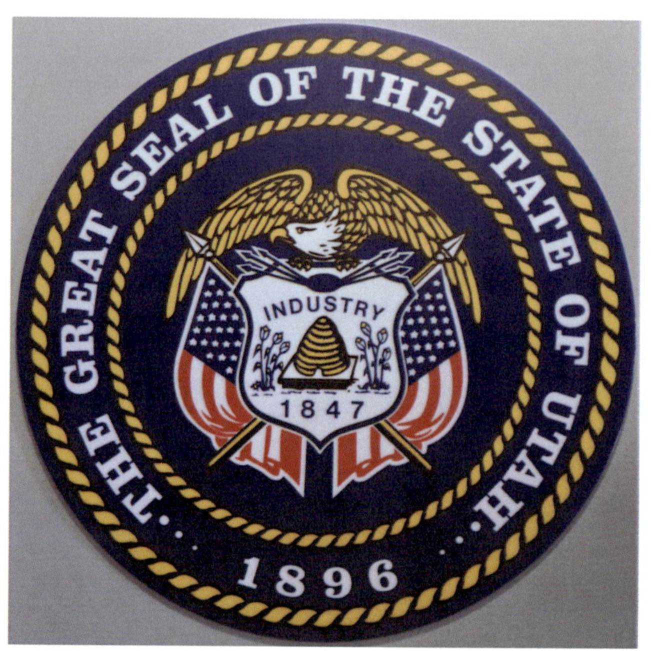

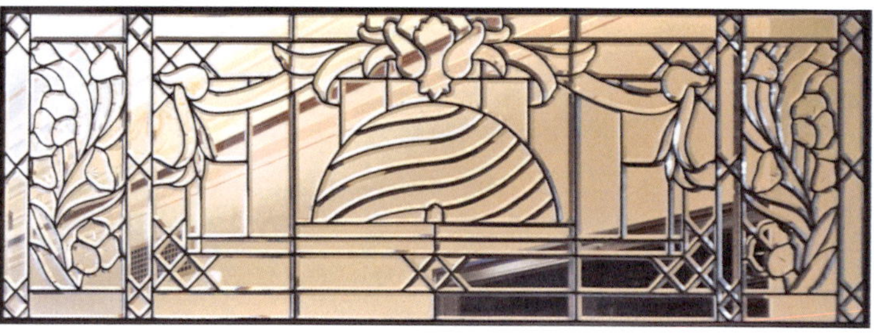

Beehive
Symbolism

Throughout the capitol grounds on the building itself, and withing the capitol's interior, are countless representations of beehives, Utah's state symbol, representing industry and cooperation.

Although the State of Deseret adopted the symbol in 1848, it wasn't until 1959 that Utah formally adopt ed it as its state symbol.

About the Photographer

Jane Moorman describes herself as an adventurer who loves to drive the backroads to see what there is to see.

During her 30-year journalism career, Jane honed her photographic skills as a photojournalist, including covering high school sporting events.

A friend once said, "I wish I could see the world as Jane sees it. Finding the beauty in things that most of us don't take time to see."

Upon retiring in 2021, Jane decided there is a lot of her native country she had not visited, including each state's capitol, so she began her journey of exploring the USA.

Jane currently lives in Albuquerque, New Mexico, but says her real home is on the road.

www.ingramcontent.com/pod-product-compliance
Lightning Source LLC
Chambersburg PA
CBRC100836110726
48006CB00009B/1418